NO BODY HOME

No Body Home

AMY DAVID

BLUE SKETCH PRESS

BLUE SKETCH PRESS
8 Mellon Terrace
Pittsburgh, PA 15206
www.bluesketchpress.com

Copyright 2015 by Amy David

All rights reserved, including right of reproduction in whole or in part or in any form.

Printed in the United States of America
9 8 7 6 5 4 3 2 1

First Printing, Blue Sketch Press Trade Paperback Edition, 2015
ISBN (print)   978-1-942547-00-6
ISBN (ebook)   978-1-942547-01-3

Cover Art by Wetsun, "The Ties That Bind."
More information available at www.flickr.com/photos/wetsun
Design by Little Owl Creative, www.littleowlcreative.com
Edited by Joseph N. Welch, III.

ACKNOWLEDGEMENTS
Some of these poems have appeared in *Drunk in a Midnight Choir, Alight: The Best Loved Poems of WOWPS 2013, Chicago Literati, The Bakery, Foundling Review, Linden Avenue Literary Journal,* and *Word Riot.*

for the survivors

Contents

Upon Lecturing a Male Friend about the Danger of Gender Role
While Simultaneously Texting Another Man About My Boobs   13
Ladybits   16
Berlin, 1944   18
Hiroshima, 1945   20
The South Dakota Badlands Talk Back to Me on My Summer Vacation   22
The Plan of Chicago   24
Circumstantial Evidence   26

What Nobody Told Me About Thirty   21
White Nights   23
Cutting the Ribbon   24
White Woman in Hong Kong   26
Snow White in Bondage   28
The Creator Over-Explains His Joke   30
Jump   31
Nerd Girl   32
Phase Transition   33
Fair Warning   34

Don't Believe Anything I Say   35
Two Things   36
On Falling in Love in July: 37
On Falling in Love in the Same Month I Ran Out of Xanax and
My Psychiatrist Refused Me a Refill: 38
Unfair Warning   39
Dispatch From the Chinese Room   40
MASH   41
On the Day Pat Quinn Told Me Not to Leave My House   42
Anyone Worth Doing is Worth Doing Madly   44

Polyphemus at the Strip Mall, or
Everything in the 7-Eleven Reminds Me of Heartache   46

Pit Bull   49
Why, She Wouldn't Even Harm a Fly   51
Help Yourself   52
Ten Things I Never Told My Father,
Yet He Still Wrote Me Out of His Will   53
Legacy 54
Cinders and All   55

The Rapist Stood Up in Court and Said   57
Punchlines   58

Acknowledgements   81
About the Author   83

NO BODY HOME

Upon Lecturing a Male Friend about the Danger of Gender Roles While Simultaneously Texting Another Man About My Boobs

Sometimes feminism is wonderfully obvious:
buy woman-made, boycott Rush Limbaugh, grow a cunt beard.

But feminism doesn't tell me what to do
about this bar full of hipsters;
I lust hard after guys in glasses and skinny jeans.

Did I just objectify an entire room full of men?
And if so...
does that bring us closer to equality?

> *Is that a glass ceiling in your pants?*
> *Because I could see myself pounding against it for the next thirty-five years.*

> *Was your father a mechanic?*
> *Then where did you get such a finely tuned sense of appropriate boundaries?*

> *If looks could kill,*
> *you'd be lucky Congress blocked the Violence Against Women Act.*

On to the small talk. Approved topics:
the Blackhawks,
the failure of charter schools,
unionization efforts at Target,
obscure craft beers, and how this place used to be so much cooler
before all the kids from Lincoln Park started coming here.

Avoid my body, his body,
what I'd like to do to his body
and anything that has ever been written in Cosmo.

By now, we need another trip to the bar:
> *Women only make 77 cents for every dollar earned by a man;*
> *can I buy you three-quarters of a drink?*
> *How about a Long Island Iced?*

I'm supposed to be "sex-positive,"
like I show up in bed with pom-poms
and motivational cat posters.

> *2-4-6-8-oral sex is really great!*
> *All of the orgasms, none of the shame!*

Too bad pop culture never got the memo:
Victoria's Secret is still selling thongs that say "Sure Thing",
and Steubenville is still blaming the victim.
How do I say sex without saying object?

> *That's a nice shirt. It would look great on my floor*
> *after we've both given enthusiastic consent.*

> *If I said you had a nice body, would you hold it*
> *at exactly the distance you feel comfortable from me?*

> *Are you pro-choice?*
> *Let's go do things that lead to abortion.*

Now for the close--does he want to leave with me?
Do I want to leave with him?
His place or mine?
Exactly how many drinks has each of us had,
divided by our weight and rates of metabolism?
Is it gender neutral for neither one of us
to be carrying a condom?

Susan B. Anthony, am I failing you,
or do you wish you'd been allowed
to have this much fun?

Ladybits

The frozen blade of daylight, the dry heaves of the alarm,
Thursday morning in someone else's bed.

I have to get out of here, I tell him, I am going to the doctor
for my ladybits exam and his face raisins in disgust,

Do you have to use that word? Fine: vag, giner, vajayjay,
sugar bowl, fish taco, box, honey pot, beaver, muff?

Deep dish, velvet tent, moist alligator, inverted clown?
Pussy, he says, *what is wrong with pussy?* Last night's

clothing leaps onto my lap and the ceiling fan is a circular
saw slicing through the regret. Pussy is a bedroom word, pussy,

like towels grabbed early from the dryer, butterscotch,
Chinese handcuffs. Pussy smokes too many cigarettes.

Pussy once bought a Chris Brown album. Pussy shuts
off the lights before dinner. It is true that we are still

in the bedroom, his hands even still on my breasts,
and yet I am not a thing that lives between the sheets.

I shop for groceries and write papers and stand
at the front of a classroom blathering on about demand

and what is it then? Paper crane, pink lunchbox, the star
of a British soap commercial, a tissue paper flower

like we made with twists of pipe cleaner and gave
to our mothers. Coffee date. Fortune cookie. A textbook

on linear algebra. It does not offer up its name. A man calls it pussy. Pussy jumps the turnstile. Pussy goes tanning.

Pussy cuts across the neighbor's lawn. Pussy
is a name unasked for. The last time I was certain

I had the right word, it was "tinky," and I still thought
that's where pee came from, before two-piece swimsuits,

before there were commandments worth breaking
and men on their knees in confession, before anyone asked

if I'd gotten fucked, instead of asking if I'd fucked, before the walk
was shameful, before it was a scandal to still be a woman

in the morning. *What belongs to you, but is used
most often by others?* Pussy writes a memoir in third person.

Pussy takes up two seats on the train. Pussy demands
a bloody mary brunch. Pussy skips out on the check.

Berlin, 1944
In a 2013 interview, Margot Woelk revealed she had been one of Hitler's food tasters during World War II.

Fifteen of us, all young and blush, perch on the kitchen bench,
        critics on opening night,
so eager to forget about our bodies. We never forget
        about our bodies. Every held breath

is a conspiracy, every double-blink a symptom, and still,
        this is luxury. Three times a day,
my face a padlock, but my tongue a double-agent. The breeze
        of celery, the radish's smirk,

Brussels sprouts pinching gutsy and green -- when did fear
        ever dull the senses? The truth:
there is never enough. I am fervid in my duty, restless
        as a flywheel, always counting down

to the fleeting kiss of the fork. Even as The Allies blockade
        all color, here: a kaleidoscope.
Am I afraid of cyanide? Show me a woman who knows
        how to open only to joy.

I've heard the rumors: the towns left glass, the living catacombs,
        the chambers blue
as drowning. But who would it save to chew with a proper
        German scowl, to deny

myself the pleasures of aroma, to take a bullet
        instead of a meal? I used to believe
there was power in refusal. Now Berlin is on fire
        and I am a faucet run dry.

One of the guards told me dying of poison

       wouldn't be that painful;
easier than choking on the British bombs, faster
       than lying among the rubble. Here,

my death would mean something. They say the last thing
       some people see of this world
are iron gates crowned with the promise, *Work*
       will make you free.

Hiroshima, 1945

What can I say that hasn't already
been said? How his hand was a slug

in mine, how he smiled once

a year, how he wore glasses
too big for his face, his ears
pushed away from his head

a couple of mangled gutters
dragging away the summer sweat.

How every day was a uniform.

I don't even remember that
day, except that it must have been
a uniform too. How I was alone

when it happened, but he wasn't,
in the third row and his pencil
sharp when the sky flashed hot

as a getaway car, so white,
for a moment they all looked

American. He wouldn't be there

when we finally understood
the exposed film, the burning

skin, the impotent rain. He wouldn't
be there for the first grass growing

across his chest, the day his voice
dropped from aluminum to steel.

Does a bomb have a mother
and if so, can she be proud? Tell her

I once had a Little Boy myself.

The South Dakota Badlands Talk Back to Me on My Summer Vacation

You claim to be from the middle of nowhere
because you grew up without cable television,
your water came from a well that sometimes
ran yellow, and calls to 911 went unanswered
if the sheriff was out to lunch, but be honest:
you had air conditioning, and a local roller rink
and an hour-and-a-half proximity to Wrigley Field.
City slicker, what do you know about the wild?
This is the stuff of legend: the lands that are bad
to cross. The sun is red wine sour and sharper
than an overlit mirror, sleeps less than the waitress
at the Starlite Truckstop, pulls the sweat out of you
like a fast one. At midday, she erases the last
of the shadow and you regret you let your hair grow
long. Nobody gets used to the temperature, they just
become forgeries. What do you know about heat?
The snakes don't know a sparrow from a finger,
a rat from a toe, your voice is the dinner bell,
your footsteps are a checkered flag. Red and
yellow kill a fellow, the hospital is an hour away.
Your cell phone is useless in these parts.
What is beautiful that isn't dangerous?
Watch your ankles, the path is too smooth,
like your hardwood flooring, smooth like your
indoor palms, smooth like your politicians.
City slicker, what do you know about America?
Nothing gets a foothold in this earth, not the pebbles,
not the grass, not the fog that settles in
like your mother-in-law on her holiday visit,
not the Lakota homesteaded out, the Ghost
Dancers circled up like a carousel, believing
God could be stronger than manifest destiny.
What do you know about crime, about massacre,

about Wounded Knee? The four cannons set out
on the points of a cross, bodies searched
like a parking lot, relocation trains coughing up
steam, a hundred fifty natives dead, medals
of honor as the bounty, this land remembers.
Nothing grows here. Call that erosion.
A week from now, you'll show off pictures
of the gullies, the canyons, the chimney rocks,
say everything in South Dakota was hard.
City slicker, what do you know about the country?

The Plan of Chicago

Mr. Burnham, my city is so small, my city
is collapsing into this train car, into the three rows
between me and the woman who got up
to hand me a tissue. I am yelling into the phone
and the southbound does not care, transit
information on the line, some poor operator
who can't hear *hospital* and *West Side*
and keeps asking me where I am now.
By the time I answer it is no longer true.
My entire city is the movement you dreamt:
railroads and harbors and bridges, highways
and six-way intersections, a woman still
is making no progress. I am making little plans,
Mr. Burnham, I haven't the luxury of magic.
I have the urban ennui of too many corporate
coffee shops and the recession-years bloom
of title loans, cash for gold, payday advances,
the good fortune of having something left to sell.
The view from below: no Grand Lakeshore,
no monuments, no sparkling cemetery
for the secrets under old Stagg Field. Your gift,
Mr. Burnham, was to see the entire city
at once, an expanding bubble on the surface
of the soap dish Midwest. We mortals can only take
in one block at a time, maybe seven we know
well, six plus the one where we stash our junk
and bodies, the rest we pass through... ants
to a sticky bounty. I have no choice but to take
directions from a minimum wageman
with an alien headset and an out-of-date map.
Every unscratched night is a victory.
Mr. Burnham, I am sorry if your blood is not stirred.
I missed the prophecy of white walls and golden

ratios, Doric columns and grand facades.
I have never trusted anything too large
or too much like sacrifice. I contain
no temples, no record heights, no eagerness
for the clock to come down. You would know it,
Mr. Burnham, if I had twenty-two stories to spare.
You gave us the vision of a park in every precinct.
The city's dogs are forever in your debt.

Circumstantial Evidence

A 64-year-old Florida woman called emergency dispatch to report medical issues, before admitting she had called because she was lonely.

She was later charged with abuse of 911.

If I'd known that loneliness was a crime, I'd have a closet
        full of jumpsuits, orange
as the ring of rust circling my thighs,
        my nails, jai alai long

and trained to pull a blade from a bar of Irish Spring. The bail money:
        a stack of Franklins, twenty
deep, in the passenger's side nightstand, the arm's reach
        so empty, good as buried

in Jimmy Hoffa's tie clip. A once-in-a-while friend buys me
        a $2 draft but the tab in his name
makes for a lousy alibi. The district attorney looks
        strangely like the first man to kiss me,

or actually, the boy, in green plaid Converse All-Stars
        atop the storm drain cover where we met
up between free swim and horseback riding. Remember
        Hi-Tops? Remember thinking

that a boyfriend would mean a better seat at the lunch table?
        Remember when it did,
for a while? That summer I learned what a hand job was,
        not from him, from the girls

in my cabin who teased Becca Markovitz for squeezing
        so hard he cried, the same boy,
but after I had told him no, or really, made Cara tell him
        while I hid on my bottom bunk, insides

pounding like a dessert spoon in the garbage disposal.
        I wonder now what became of him,
the boy with an Israeli accent, the innocent stand-in
        for every re-corked bottle, every joke

that didn't get a laugh, every morning violently stripped of its
        colored coat. Of course I wonder, now
that I find myself untouched, not in the way that means
        I'm always on time, or the way

that gets me auctioned off to some magnate
        from a country with a shortage of brides,
but the way that turns memory into the exact change
        I need for a can of Diet Coke, the way

I keep checking the fuse box when all of the lights are on,
        the way I late-night cradle a stuffed
bear who in turn cradles a velvet heart stamped with those
        three obvious words never said

by the man who gave it to me. 3am smells like milk gone
        just a tiny bit sharp and hurled anyway
down the sink. I am a vegan's steak knife, a teetotaler's flask,
        the wristwatch on a death row prisoner.

What Nobody Told Me About Thirty

is that I'd already have friends who are dead
and my own knees would be crooning along
to Etta James. I haven't ever understood

when I am supposed to change
my shoes or split infinitives but at this age,
there are cold toes and obvious smirks.

Some days I am made of ice cream
and others I remember the Maine, only
my casing tells the truth: I can no longer

digest lies or rocky planets and the night
lights halo into dust storms. My body is
forgiving, or giving, or giving out, it has

even been given away and still. I have
walked backwards through seventeen
mirrors and cannot mend a single crack.

Most household dust is just dead skin.
I cannot control where my body lands.
My body contains fifty-three pounds of fat,

three more than the postal service will deliver
to Mexico and enough to burn for five months
two weeks and a day under the watch

of a man named Ishmael. There are things
inside me like cavities and ulcers and my adult
teeth grew in behind the first ones. I was

a shark, two rows, until the babies were metal-

tooled out of me. A bump on the back
of my head stayed for almost two weeks

before I discovered it was a wood tick.
I often pinch the side of my thigh
between my thumb and first finger and score it

with the nail on my other hand. The skin turns
slightly white and then recolors, the real thing, red
as the Martian's camouflage. I can't remember

if having these fantasies makes me crazy
or if resisting them makes me sane. I am thirty
years old and will never have nice legs. I once

promised a boy I tasted like bubble gum,
and when his teeth dropped into my shoulder, I saw
Hollywood. If only he'd had flatter arches, if only

the doorknob had stuck, if only I was a black belt
in Feng Shui. The big ones said I could
be one of them and every poster

was covered in stars. The stars are dying
too, but some will swallow whole galaxies
as they go and thousands of years

will pass before anyone notices they are
missing. No, not missing, just gone,
and who is left to clean out the fridge?

White Nights

Arrogant enamel, you boast of grinding meat and ripping open
bags of drug store liquorice, halting x-rays, bloodying lips,

how quickly you fall into ruin. None of the obvious: carrot,
lemonade, nougat, but two fire ants humping away inside

a decaying molar, eggs and larvae carving out homes in that tooth
and the next one. I cannot chew but to be stung

one thousand times on the roof, and brushing brings out the bold
ones to surf on the foam. My first weapon is coffee, burnt

and bitter, I swish it around making the faces of a blowfish
and a prude. I roll the r's in "mermaid" and "garden," but shrewd

intruders know how to burrow deep, untouchable by funnels
and flooding, I work from an angle. Lost, the brilliance of gel

and baking soda, lips pulled tight, tiny insects, listen: choose
your own way to go, this is the revolution, just one drink.

Cutting the Ribbon

It is true that plastic heels make my legs look leggier
and that pantyhose disguise some of the cellulite
appearing on my thighs--
chunky peanut butter spread across really white bread.

This does not excuse the silliness
of wearing them with a bikini
carefully attached to my body with Elmer's glue stick,
because the only thing worse than falling on your face
is cameltoe.

This is the advice I get from last year's Miss Illinois,
and with her size-five feet and constellation smile,
it is easy to believe her,
that the worst thing
in her life is a beauty pageant judge
being able to make out the shape of her vagina.

She has sponsors just for being beautiful. For five
hundred dollars she will sign a photograph
for her dentist, thanking him for the gorgeous smile,
so he can hang it in his waiting room
beside the poster about bleaching your teeth
for all the girls who want to be exactly like her.

I am seventeen, and I am one of them.

I don't care about the scholarship to junior college,
I want that crown

with rhinestones that sparkle like evidence,
and a title: Miss Chicago or Miss Northeastern Suburbs
or Miss Southern Third of the Cook County Forest Preserve.

I want the life where tragedy is a couple hairs
sticking out of the bottom of my swimsuit.

But there are nine other women in my way,
and I am the only one who reeks of french fries.

The veterans are friendly backstage,
teaching me how to inflate my hair with trouser socks
and draw in four-pack ab muscles with eyeliner.
They tell me to focus all of my eye contact
on the male judges, and help me tuck in the tags
on the designer gown I plan to return Monday morning.

The interviewer asks, *Do pageants empower women?*

They put women on the same footing as men
who want to be International Mr. Leather.
They give women opportunities they wouldn't otherwise have:
cutting the ribbon for a strip mall in central Kansas,
or circling the state in a pink SUV
delivering critical social platforms
violence is bad
and *animals are good*
and *experts still aren't certain about mammograms.*

Before the talent section begins, the dancers stretch,
the violinists tune, the singers sip, and I regret
that I never learned how to juggle fire or swallow swords.

White Woman in Hong Kong

Two girls on the Kowloon subway point
at me and one of them giggles "Godzilla."
I try to shrug away my size, elbows in,
no shoving, I very politely miss my stop.

I visit the temple of the seafaring goddess
and cannot read a single sign. A priest panics
at me, making sounds like dirty laundry
as my camera keeps flashing at the altar.

My cell phone is as useless as Betamax
and my laptop won't charge in a type G wall,
I can't rent ice skates big enough to cover
my glide, I can't walk more than five feet

in the jade market without someone grabbing
for my hand. I can spot a fake, even as the seller
flicks a lighter to the elephant necklace
she says I can pay for in U.S. dollars.

A giant billboard outside McD's shows an ad
for Madame Tussauds. None of the figures
are familiar, wax or otherwise, they look
like nobody I know, or even see on television.

Even here, the channels flip from Harry Potter
to Dr. Phil. The travel guide says to try
the French toast. Restaurants are almost clean
enough to trick me into drinking from the tap.

I stop into a rawhide lounge offering Chinese
foot massage and find out the hard way
that torture would be the kinder term. I bite my lip

like a roach clip, but stay for the entire hour.

I know exactly four words of Cantonese,
picked up from a placemat. In the drug store,
I have to pantomime hairdryer: whoooosh.
It's even worse when I need tampons.

And in the aisle for face wash, every bottle
is marked whitening formula. Someone,
everyone, is envious of this flaky crust, overbaked
in the forced heat of thirty-one Chicago winters.

Every tailor on Mody Road says I have
such long legs, they'll have to charge me
fifty for a custom suit. Women rush up to ask
if I need a maid or a Western-style haircut.

The Coach store is disguised as a shanty.
Back at the station, I have no money
for the subway. The ticket machine
only takes coins. I only have large bills.

Snow White in Bondage
After Daphne Gottlieb

A girl this fair cannot
marry anyone
but a prince,
said Mr. Disney,
said the Brothers Grimm,
they told me that's
what I want, that's
what every girl wants.
I'm the purest
in the land, I'd be crazy
not to wait
for Mr. Charming.
But I was never
a woman who wanted
one true love,
not when I had
Doc, who'd perch
his specs on the tip
of his ruddy nose
and examine me
real good, the latex
gloves squeaking
down my back.
Grumpy, demanding
I lick his floppy
brown boots,
yes master,
I've been a bad girl,
yes, tell
the huntsman
where I am hiding,
the safeword

is "happily ever after."
Dopey, in diapers,
his pacifier
sucked
so hard
as he crawled
to my milk,
Happy and Sleepy,
always blissfully
high, damn,
did those two
make me work.
Sneezy, poor
thing, allergic
to all that fur,
and Bashful,
what a joke it was,
calling him that,
the man who'd do it
in a church pew,
who'd wear nothing
but a trench coat
to Millennium Park,
how he liked to see
his cock
wave down
from its reflection
in the Bean.
I should have
turned him down
when he insisted
we hang a mirror
from the ceiling,
but how was I
to know it was

such a snitch?
There was no
haze of magic,
just a better view
of my fair, fair ass
bobbing
like a lost buoy.
The apple, too,
looked ordinary,
no idol shine
or devilish smirk,
no hint its flesh
would expel me
from Paradise.
I didn't even mind
the glass coffin,
centering the circle
jerk, seven
ruddy knobs
all pointed at my
untouchable face,
but the rescue,
that over-bleached
hair and cloud
of Axe Body Spray:
not charming at all.

The Creator Over-Explains His Joke

The green eyes were mostly a prank
I played on your mother. Believe it or not
she was sober back then and your neighborhood
didn't even have a milkman. I'm sorry
they don't see so well at night, and when you flash them
angry against a mirror you see their color
souring to lime, but your entire life
men will say they are beautiful
and you will know better
than to stand in that kind of line.
A lover you don't love
will see them as a highway exit sign
with a meaningless number and a name
found in every small town, he'll remind you
that you're Third or Fourth and that you never run
on an angle. Another will tell you
they remind him of a Heineken
and it won't be a compliment, exactly,
or really at all, but it will be the most honest
thing ever said about your parts.

Jump

After nine-and-a-half days as a Domino's delivery driver,
I slit my wrists with a pizza cutter. My first week as a cashier,
I overdosed on nickels. I tried waiting tables for a while,
but you can guess how that ended up: apron strings
pulled tight around my neck. My cubicle job lasted almost
six weeks before I put a PowerPoint bullet through my brain.
I made beds in a five-star hotel until the penthouse balcony
proved to be a platform of temptation. That was the most fun,
I admit. There is no clearer view of the city than the one
seven seconds from certain death. Gold Coast windows
flash by like a flipbook: the marbled bathroom complete
with bidet and a toilet-top television. The wet bar stocked
with Vox and Cristal. The abstract masterpiece hung
upside-down above the Italian leather sofa. Someone
should market this to tourists: "Plunge into the Good Life!"
"Be your own guide!" The only sightseeing tour that ends
without anyone hitting you up for a tip. I've had it backwards
my entire life. When someone said *jump*, I would ask
how high? But all it really takes is a belly-flop into luxury, bank
on your bone structure or family name or let your god decide
who gets the soft landing. My god is gravity. I am a gumball
at the turn of a dial, hoping only to jam the machine. The busboy
drops one too many curses. The deckhand plots to steal the regatta
wind. The man with a garbage bag briefcase can ride
the train for days on a single fare. This is the closest he gets
to resistance. No chants, no signs, no megaphones,
the squeaky wheel gets fleeced. If you cannot be force,
be friction. If you have no voice, vibrate. If you cannot stop
the race to the bottom, at least cause some chafing. There is
no ancient Chinese text on the Art of Class Warfare,
but the busker on Washington and LaSalle gets louder
every time he sees a necktie. The girl in the field licks

every berry she yanks from the vine. She loves the taste
of pesticide and she knows she'll die young anyway.

Nerd Girl

glasses / headgear / Mickey Mouse sweatshirt / tapered jeans / original hipster / underwear showing / middle school / high school algebra / very own bus / picked last / B in gym class / imperfect GPA / before nerds were cool / nerd friends / no friends / no dates / school dance / can't dance / running man / pretty dress / everyone else in jeans / honors science / only girl / no partner / do slinky lab alone / wrong wavelength / physics joke / correct teacher's spelling / bookstore / want everything / Go Ask Alice / want LSD / too chicken / D.A.R.E. / snowflake / after school special / Bat Mitzvah / forty-two invitations / thirty-five RSVPs / twenty-three no-shows / tiny hora / summer camp / queer boy / Russian girl / fat girl / really weird clique / hiking / camp songs / multitask / out of breath / back to school / campsick / strep throat / stay home / antibiotic / thirty pills / skip ten on purpose / strep throat / stay home / flat chest / asked to play ping pong / can't help it / skipped grades / locker room / surrounded / talk back / outnumbered / bruises / scratches / missing hair / nosy mother / blame eyesight / glasses

Phase Transition

White dwarf, still glowing at fifteen million degrees,
your fuel is gone. A lifetime of fusion halts, you are
nothing inside. Dead star. You are the last flickers
of the core, cooling to dirt and ash, wishing you
were somebody's home. Next door you feel the pull
of an entire galaxy, its two exquisite arms spiraling
out to hug you, but you know this is a false gesture.
You know you will never be in the same galaxy as
the popular stars, the ones orbited by more planets
than they can possibly warm at once. You watch
from afar the prom queen, the one with even Pluto
fighting for a spot in her entourage. The third of her
admirers, you've heard, is old and balding, but he
wins favor by watching her pets. You are jealous,
not of the number, but of the newness that appears
every time he turns around. When the decision is made
to send you his humans past their prime, you briefly feel
hope in your neutrons. The first migrants are the ones
who burned out waiting for the Messiah. They made
arrangements for the atheists to feed their dogs
after the rapture, spent all their money on a giant cross
in the desert, and picked out the perfect witty t-shirts
to fall to the floor where they stood at midnight,
December 31, 2999. They are not good colonists, owing
to that they are mostly Americans, and don't know
a thing about sacrifice. The first winter is the hardest
for them, being that it lasts forever, and there is no
native population to destroy then celebrate by drawing
hand-turkeys, nor can they keep warm by wallowing
in their hatred of the British. Still, they get by, hanging
around the event horizon and sucking up matter, always
muttering the 23rd psalm, and you, dark star, lie still
in your pajamas, bracing for another couple millennia.

Fair Warning

No man who has loved me
should think of me in the bathtub
without fearing electrocution.

No man who has screamed my name
should call his broker
to buy more stock.

No man who remembers pulling my hair
should ride a roller coaster
next to a stranger.

I will laugh the first time
you see me naked. I will step
on your toes to get closer.

I will make love to you
in funny socks. I will leave you
all of the purple jelly beans.

I am not a flame but the candle
dripping wax. I am not a sad note
but the hammer that hits it.

Love Dobermans instead
or crossword puzzles.
Find a wife who lets you lie

in her bed with the real
estate section. Search for
a townhouse with a spiral staircase.

And if I appear there one morning like Jesus
on the toast of a believer,
it is nothing a butter knife won't fix.

Don't Believe Anything I Say

The truth is the crescent moon
was a toenail clipping

and some careless celestial smoker
had burned stars into the corduroy sky.

The truth is there was no music.
We danced to the garbage can rustle.

The wine was cheap and the waitress
cheaper. The truth is promises are a treadmill.

My six-year-old-self dreamt of life
in a castle. The truth is the hummingbirds

are drunk. You wink like a filmstrip
and turntable in your sleep and missing

you feels like always needing to pee,
but anything that could melt

in my mouth doesn't belong in my hands.
When I think about you now,

I have had it with poems
about the smell of rain.

Two Things

Most schoolchildren recall two things
about Helen Keller: she was deaf, and
she was blind. The woman who read
with her hands. In the movie shown
to third-graders, she does not even get
the title role. We mute the television,
wander out at midnight, box our ears
and close our eyes like this is all it takes
to imagine. My sister's silhouette never
appeared on the back of a quarter. She
was bald, and she was breastless. A
pink ribbon on a now-oversized sweater.
In the oncology ward, she did not even
get to wear her favorite slippers. I leave
my hair for the dustpan, draw tread marks
down my chest, press them against me
and strain my neck downward to make
certain they bounce back, bounce back.

On Falling in Love in July:

All of the clichés are true: the birds are singing outside every window, there is a lump in my throat like chocolate dark as drowning, and my thighs that aren't in shape for a mini-skirt suddenly look good in a mini-skirt.

On Falling in Love in the Same Month I Ran Out of Xanax and My Psychiatrist Refused Me a Refill:

It is 5am and the birds are chirping like a hyperactive car alarm, pigeons, probably, or some other breed that shits on everything, and I don't know if breed is the right word for kinds of birds like pigeon and I keep trying out other words in my head, type, category, genre, none of them fit and my laptop is in the other room and once I get out of bed it's all over, I don't have to be up until 8am but the fucking birds, the fucking birds, pecking at my brain stem: he's going to leave you, he's going to leave you, he's going to leave you. There is a lump in my throat that is all post-nasal drip and moves from side to side depending on which way I hit the pillow, my air-conditioner only coughs in two settings: mucus-making, and sub-Saharan Africa, and I've chosen snot over sweat, and my thighs, they're fat, alright, they always have been, and always will be, and nobody will ever love this body.

Unfair Warning

If you let a poet love you, beware
that you will be responsible

for reckless misuse
of the ocean and countless lies

about the moon. The weight of infatuation
will curve your spine into a cliché.

You will come to know the color
of your own hair with quartz precision,

and how the shadows
of a single strand move with the hour.

He will set your body down
on the page as an umbrella, make gates

of your eyes, know intimately
the cursive loops of your name.

You will never be seen as soft
or sloppy, nearsighted and afraid

of fireworks. He will write you
flat as an inkblot, an empty margin.

Here is a lover who will seduce you
in search of a manuscript,

bring you tulips only when
he can steal the chatter of their bloom.

Dispatch From the Chinese Room

In an effort to prove I am not a zombie, I wash my hair
with 7Up and eat shredded newsprint for breakfast.
For every rule of human behavior, there are five
more rules on when to break it. My body sneezes
without consulting me, laughs and vomits and sweats.
I give myself paper cuts so I can feel pain, and then think
about the pain, and then later on, remember that
I have thought about the pain. It is helping me build up
a tolerance for small stings, until the day comes
that I dissect myself, looking for a reaction, chemical.

MASH
After Franny Choi

You will live in a
mansion/apartment/shack/house
and marry
Jon Hamm/Ryan Gosling/George Clooney/Mick Jagger
and live in
Paris/Las Vegas/New York City/Schaumburg
and drive a
Ferrari/Jaguar/Lamborghini/Shopping cart
to your job as a
supermodel/brain surgeon/rock star/nun
then come home to your
one/two/three/twenty-five children.

***

You will live in a
mansion/apartment/shack/house
and marry
your hot coworker/the cute barista/my brother/your brother
and live in
Noble Square/Lincoln Square/Lincoln Park/Wicker Park
and drive a
Lexus/Prius/Smart Car/Segway
to your job as a
sales rep/coder/manager/accountant
then come home to your
twins/dog/daughter/five kids.

***

You will live in an
apartment/apartment/apartment/apartment
and marry
some guy you met at the Mutiny/a friend of a friend/nobody/an OKCupid date

in
Humboldt Park/Rogers Park/Logan Square/Avondale
and drive a
used car/used bike/used motorcycle/Ventra
to your job as a
teacher/bartender/student/writer
then come home to your
journal/decaf/PlayStation 4/empty bed

On the Day Pat Quinn Told Me Not to Leave My House

Chicago is known for its fire, not the water
that put it out, but today, the city has gone biblically

wicked: my basement is an aquarium of third grade
report cards, the hydrant is suffocating, and a woman

got a DUI just for leaving her driveway.
The newsheads spin with panic: people die

like this, their cars suddenly swamped, the front door
a tackling sled for the currents, the sinkhole

at 95th and Houston an entire block of surrender.
The man I know is about to leave me thinks this

is the prettiest it has ever been. Gone
are the differences between concrete

and cement and how each one can be used
by a man. He is smug about his escape, excited

by rats waving up from the sewers, certain
he is smarter than the surge. This is not a man

who can love a sidewalk that only gets him
to the right place: the fifth square marked

with shallow letters that meant something
to someone else, the seventh pocked

with two weak dots above the curved flick
of a smile, the gentle puddle that asks him to take

three steps into the street, the hesitant curb
or the brittle moment when the right foot lords above

the left. No, this is man who needs to be knee-deep
in disruption, the rip tiding into his boots, the invited pain

of standing on his own wrinkled toes.
He wants the torrent, the burst, the rush

of rain overloading the city like a sour chord
blowing out an amp, the scatter of the surface

at footfall, and the way he really believes
he could convince this flood to stay.

Anyone Worth Doing is Worth Doing Madly

When you told me it was over, the bedsheets tumbled
inside-out on the mattress and the hot water

bill tripled in a single day. I put your lips in a jar
and marked them for sale with a sign that said Gently Used

and Sometimes Roughly Used, set
the asking price at thirty-one doubts

or best offer and got the chance to fit back into
my skinny jeans. I told myself that you are doing

even worse, it's an easy lie, but one
with spurs: this is me you are talking to,

this can still work. Let me turn all the clocks
forward an hour and hand you the daylight.

Say which inch of me sounds like a minor key,
I will tune myself black and blue. The book of poems

you gave back to me is even worse
for the wear, barreled into your pocket, yielding

spine, at least you once said you loved it. I knew
you would, like I knew you'd chew through

the brake lines. Dummy, I failed the crash test. I have
no right to be this parceled. We didn't even make it

through a pack of birth control, the life
of a mealworm, the money-back guarantee

on a new set of tires. I am pretending that it started
when you asked, that we were hand-drawn

in all the months before, and even harder
I am pretending we will be again: flat

and with obvious edges. Did you know when
they animate a character, they only draw her

torso once? It saves time that way, to slap on
different limbs and twistings of her face

so she can lindy hop and gossip and fuck and sob
but the core of her never changes. I meant

it when I told you I'd do it all over again: the lost
hours of dreaming, Christmas Eve shivering

with anger, the shoes that were practically
never worn, and still, the meteor shower,

that first night together on the beach, waiting
in twenty degree wind-chill for something

to flash across the sky; I wanted you so badly
to believe me. And when the first point of light

finally tore through the midnight canvas,
it was an opening for the two of us alone.

I said the Hebrew prayer for creation.

Polyphemus at the Strip Mall
or
Everything in the 7-Eleven Reminds Me of Heartache

A pint of cherry chocolate chip ice cream
in a generic green container,
the flavor identifiable
only by the white text.
It's the same
as Ben and Jerry's,
a lie I tell myself
to save
thirty-nine cents.

Nobody told
the raspberry Slurpee
it shouldn't be blue.

Wiper fluid.
Coolant.
Anti-freeze.
All useless
without a funnel.
An empty spot
where the funnels
used to be.
Would five minutes
have mattered?
Fifteen? An hour?
Timing is everything or
timing is nothing or
timing is an arbitrary construct
that keeps the pain
from hitting
all at once.

Cigarettes.
A new law on cigarettes.
The gold pack is no longer
labeled lights
but you ask for them
by saying you want lights.
I don't ask for them.
I quit cold turkey.
Another lie.
I quit
by swapping cigarettes
for psych meds.

Actual cold turkey.
Who decided flesh
doesn't need to be warm
if it is instead
sliced thin
as a bootstrap?

More flesh:
Hot dogs on the rotisserie
keep turning
towards each other
but never touch,
or hot dogs on the rotisserie
keep turning
away from each other
but never escape.

Travel size packets of everything.
Condoms in threes,
but aspirins by the pair.
Don't we all want

to get fucked
more than we want
to get better?

Individual razors.
Where is my ambition?
Gillette Mach 3.
Triple the speed of sound.
If they were really that fast,
I might not resist.

Lottery tickets.
Not the standard cliché
about lottery tickets.
Nothing about instants
or set for life.
No luck.
But no desperation, either.
Maybe how violently
you scratch at their skin
and there's always
another one to be bought.

An extension cord.
Go farther away
but do the same thing.

One day I'll learn
the name of that neon magazine
is not U.S. Weekly.
Us. Me and you.
Weekly. Weakly.
Just a tabloid.
Just an escape.

Three ATMs.
Seven kinds of Kit-Kat.
Twelve daily newspapers.
The luxury of options.
The burden of choosing.

Pit Bull

Dog-sitting in January means five-minute walks, wind-chill
like the nose of a ghost. When the thermostat finally jumps

above the drinking age, it a day for the dog park. What a relief
to finally be off-leash. A woman shows up with a full-size poodle-

looking dog, dirty white and royal, and Ripley is curious,
then growling, and the poodle howls back. They sniff and roll,

the poodle on top of Ripley, and by the time I yank at his collar,
both dogs are back on their feet, Ripley's jaws mousetrapped

onto the side of the other dog's face. The owner is screaming
and trying to pull her dog away, and I have my hands on his neck

but Ripley cannot let go. The UPS man sees us, runs in, straddles
him and grabs at his ears like handlebars and still he can't let go,

and Ripley, it's January, and I'm hurting, I can't let go, he
dumped me, and I can't let go. There are three or four people gathered

around now and the owner yells to call the police, and he just
keeps clamping down, and this is what I do, Ripley, I'm so bad

at letting go. Someone has a broomstick, swatting him in the face
and there are people pulling on both sides and my dog doesn't

care, those teeth never let up and I am a poet, Ripley, and poets
practically invented heartache, but we never mastered it, never

learned how to exile it to the page. Sometimes we all hope
too hard, cling too long to a mouthful of bloody fur. I could never

love a man who won't sleep in the woods, Ripley, and I knew
better, and the owner is still making a noise like dental floss

and I'm afraid to jerk the collar too hard. I've been acting helpless,
Ripley, and I am not helpless, though I sometimes lack strength

in my upper body, and nobody else is going to come along
and fix it, it has to be me, straight for the eyes, and I can't even

do it with the tips of my fingers, I have nails, Ripley, I promise
this will be quick, my slapstick knuckles, and it's enough to shock

the dogs apart and everyone is still yelling at me and outside
the gate I have to sit down, and there is blood beneath his eyes,

and three-pointed craters, and maybe the poodle bit first
but it doesn't matter, if they both hurt each other,

nobody will ever remember it that way, and everyone is still
yelling but one winter-pink woman tells me you're not a bad dog,

Ripley, you just got scared. You did what anyone would do.

Why, She Wouldn't Even Harm a Fly
After Rebecca Hoogs

Every horror film has that one woman who is much too pretty
to be there, some college student played by an actress old enough
to have walked like an Egyptian, with breasts like over-baked
cupcakes, and hair that belongs at Madame Tussauds.
The character is a cheerleader, or student council president,
and you know she is popular because she drives a red convertible.

I'm the other one. The one whose character development consists
entirely of the fact that I'm wearing glasses, the one who gets
about three witty lines, two fewer than the weightlifting bro who
will be deli meat twenty minutes in because he just had to go get
another beer from the cooler in the obviously haunted garage,
but still more screen time than the token black guy. It starts

out in a bar, in February, so the moon is early, the sidewalks are ripe
for falling, and there is nothing weird about meeting a man
who drinks his beer from under a ski mask. I'm the character
who thinks it's cute when he says he loves me two weeks in,
it's heroic and cinematic that he wants to spend every night
with me, and I can't hear all the screaming from the rows of velvet seats,

"don't go there!" "it's dangerous!" I am off
swimming alone in the dark, wearing heels in the forest,
collecting strange antiques. I can't see the audience
shaking their heads, wondering how I can be so oblivious
that the bad guy is right there in my apartment and my friends
are mysteriously disappearing. I'm alone with a man who leaves gifts

on my wrists, who tells me nobody else will ever want me, my friends
have left me on purpose, and my family doesn't notice I'm gone.
The dramatic irony is that I believe him. From the inside, I can't see
the ominous fog settling in and the music's slow climb to a crescendo.

The screen is so dark the exit signs glow like fire trucks, but the cliché isn't earned: remember Act I? Wasn't I supposed to be the smart one?

Help Yourself

Our bedroom became a quiet zone between the hours
of midnight and midnight. The day I started calling

you my partner, you must have heard half of everything.
The left breast: yours, the hand that doesn't write: yours,

you said poetry hadn't been important since Pound.
As a token of the times we catgut whack-a-moled

on the steaming clay, I will even let you have the good
knee. When I came home from the doctor hugging a jar

of lemons, you wouldn't even unscrew the lid, now take
them all, every last pimpled fruit. Half of the stomach

that won't digest milk: yours. Half of the Ambien addiction:
yours. Half of the unfilled cavities, half of the cellulite

I've only heard of second-hand, half of the nighttime vision
so bad I have mistaken my lovers for lovers: yours,

yours, yours. There is a pile started on your nightstand;
you can form words with my unlocked jaw: please, more,

yes. Take one of the scars where a pencil went through both
sides of my hand, the jammed fourth finger, all of the taste

buds for bitter. Nobody ever loved me harder
than you did, never more like a canyon. When the sunset

weeps a thousand brilliant pinks, it means the smog is choking.
Take half of my throat. Stuff it full of every moan you saved

up from the good years. Listen to them sneaking away
like the air from a bitten tire, just as the rest of me is waking.

Ten Things I Never Told My Father, Yet He Still Wrote Me Out of His Will

1. My therapist once warned me that you could get sober and still be an asshole. You got cancer and were still an asshole. You refused to see a therapist to talk about the fact you were dying; I guess that makes you macho. Also dead.

2. Every time you asked why I didn't make Homecoming Court equated to roughly three men I slept with as a teenager. My high school nickname was pincushion.

3. As a child, I use to fantasize about you dying, though not so painfully as you actually did. I always thought it would be a heart attack or an overdose, never cancer. I can't remember if I understood life insurance, or if I just thought we'd be better off poor.

4. Before introducing you to my boyfriend, I bet him twenty dollars you would ask him if he didn't prefer me with longer hair. I should have gone double-or-nothing on contact lenses.

5. When you were dating Christine, her daughter took me to a party, and I liked her so much I told her Christine could find someone better. When it got back to you later, I said I had been drinking, which fortunately excused everything in your book. I hadn't been drinking.

6. We all knew you would die in December. You hated the holidays, accused everyone of being fake kind, said people who couldn't be bothered eleven months out of the year were suddenly filling up the bell ringer's cup. I would never call you an honest man but I'll give you this: when you didn't want to be nice to someone, you simply weren't.

7. I tried to explain to my friend Sarah why I didn't speak to you for five years. I rambled all the way from Providence to Boston, and the best I came up with was the time you smacked me for dropping the

transmission. You apologized that same night, though, and I told her that too.

8. This is how I should have explained you: you never let me lock the bathroom door.

9. The best memory I have is the time you came to visit me in Champaign, when we went to Legends and drank pitchers of Coors Light and spent the whole night tapping people on the shoulder and then pretending it wasn't us when they turned around to look. You were right: sometimes it's a lot of fun to be drunk and mean.

10. I did not tell that story at your funeral. I read someone else's poem about her father being drunk at a ballgame. I changed the word "Wrigley" to "Comiskey" and everyone said it was perfect and everyone was right. You would have hated it. You wouldn't have even pretended otherwise.

Legacy

What I mean by legacy:
    when I look up, I see Orion
  loosening his belt. There is no chance of hiding
      above ground. I am an earthworm on asphalt.

    When I look up, I see the Hunter.
I study my feet, such silly things keep me
      above ground. I am an earthworm on asphalt.
  I keep trying to build a moat.

I study my feet. Such silly things keep me
    spiraling forward, then… Back to the man who made me:
  I keep trying to build a moat,
      but the past has wings. This is

    spiraling, forward then back, to the man who made me
loosen his belt. There is no chance of hiding
      when the past has wings. This is
          what I mean by legacy.

Cinders and All

My parents bought a house alongside the highway
just to watch it burn. The fire chief lit the match
himself. We sat in my brother's convertible
in a lot across the street and I tried to capture it
all on 110mm film. This is not the whole story.

My parents bought a house alongside the highway
because the property was supposed to be
some kind of investment, but the house
had gone grey and smelled like a clogged sink,
and one time my father took me down to the basement
and pretended the lights were broken so I had
to hold on to him really tightly just to get back
up the stairs. This is not the whole story.

One time my father took me down to the basement
and pretended I was the crawl space, too small
for an adult, but sometimes useful as a place
to stash your shame. The exterminator hadn't been
in that cellar for years and the only thing keeping rats
away was the mildew. My mother stayed out of it, too,
claimed she had the same allergies I did, but tried
to plant ferns in the yard. This is not the whole story.

My mother stayed out of it, too, sat at the chipper desk
in our real house, the one with stark white walls
that stayed clean for eleven years, didn't think
about the way things fade when you abandon them.
I had seen it in that basement, everything
falling apart, worse: everything exposed, the tile
cracked like a grandmother, the insulation confettied
across the floor. I could have finger sparked
the copper wire. This is not the whole story.

I could have finger sparked that house
to the ground but the fire chief beat me to it.
They called it a training drill, thanked my parents
for the donation, got the whole squad suited up
for a Saturday morning scrimmage. Not one
of the men looked clenched as they threw it
to the flames. This is not the whole story.

They threw it to the flames. I was eleven
and terrified of heat. I didn't know destruction
could be so eager and every time I thought the fire
was done, again, it would raise its arms in prayer.
I wanted it all on film, but in the pictures, there are
only storm clouds, the blaze muffled and grey.
Nobody would believe the inferno, the way that house
charred itself into me. Nobody would believe
the whole story. My parents would never admit
they burned their own house to the ground.

The Rapist Stood Up in Court and Said
After Jeffrey McDaniel

I am not a rapist. I dreamt those women were icebergs
who needed my help. Before you judge me,
consider what becomes of the dripping:
how just a few drops provoke the tornado sirens,
how a sprinkle is enough to scare
the turtle back into his shell. I am the first man
to bend spoons with my voice. Can I help it
if bodies follow? You've never seen
how they dangle, each one the corner
of a Band-Aid come unstuck. You've never
been there when they fan themselves out
in front of me. Pick a card, any card.
I am not a criminal for pulling the queen
from the deck. Do you blame the worm
for the fishhook? Do you attack the rake
for the leaves? Your honor, I am certain
she came onto me. Your honor, I am certain
she came. The laws of anatomy dictate
that every human smile is a wet one.
You call me wicked, but have you ever seen
an unemployed carousel, a lonely apple pie,
fireworks with nobody watching?
You know how you become famous?
One admirer at a time. You can't have poetry
without line breaks, a spotlight without shadows,
an audience without fools. Ladies and gentlemen
of the jury, this is the first time in decades
I have spoken to so little applause.
I barely remember how to say my lines
with nobody chanting along. I am bigger
than this costume, bigger than this flourish, bigger
than this act of creation. I get on stage

to build a canon all my own. What grander finale
than a woman sawn in half? Ask any critic:
what good is an artist who won't violate
boundaries? Who would choose truth
when they could have four-star reviews?
Watch them all lining up to be my lovely assistants.
See how I've dressed them in disappearing silks?
See how I've painted their mouths shut?

Punchlines

A pamphlet distributed on my college campus tells women
to yell out "I have AIDS" while being raped,
 in the hopes of scaring off the rapist.

When this did not deter the man on top of me,
I yelled out, "I have high cholesterol,"
"I have sudden infant death syndrome,"
"I have a tendency to spontaneously combust,"
"I have a fleshlight in my purse."

This was a "date rape,"
which is to say, I knew the perpetrator,

and nobody wants to bother dividing the statistics into
"classmate who doesn't brush his teeth but yawns like he does" rape,
"guy in yoga class who takes staff pose literally" rape,
"dude at the coffee shop who is either suspicious
or just too into Arcade Fire" rape and
"bartender who keeps giving me free shots even though I am only seventeen
years old and nobody should drink Goldschläger at any age" rape.

This is bullshit, if we're gonna call it "date rape,"
I demand dinner and a movie!
And fuck it, I'm ordering popcorn.
And junior mints.
And a soda so big, I'll need yo mama's stretchpants for a koozie.
I'm ordering red hots and hot tamales and atomic fireballs;
you stick your dick in my mouth, it's coming out sunburned.

I'm sure some defense attorney will ask
why I didn't put habaneros in my vagina,
make bearded clam into bearded clamato,
rooster sauce my ass

and my nose, my ears, my armpits,
and the inside of my fingers when I make a fist.

The hospital bill read as follows:
Physical evidence recovery kit (rape kit): $472
Professional services: $180
Emergency contraception: $42
Who knew sexual violence came with so many hidden fees?
You'd think my rapist worked for Citibank.

Joke's on me, though,
student insurance didn't cover anything!
Approximate number of hours worked at a minimum-wage
retail job to pay for my own rape kit: 97,
but wouldn't it be a riot if I changed the number and told you it was 69?
Wouldn't it be twice as funny if I got raped a second time?
Or the hattrick, the threepeat,
Michael Jordan and the '93 Bulls got nothing on me.
Nah, preventing rape is as easy as preventing mail fraud:
never let anyone near your box.

Three years later, on a visit to Champaign,
two men cornered me in a bar to tell me I'd accused their friend of rape.
This was funny, because
    1. I already knew this
    2. I could now accuse them of accusing me
       of accusing their friend of rape
       and we could go on like this forever
    3. They weren't even laughing.

Acknowledgements

Thank you to the editors of the following publications in which versions of these poems have appeared:

Upon Lecturing a Male Friend [...]	Alight: The Best Loved Poems of WOWPS 2013
Berlin, 1944	Chicago Literati
The Creator Over-Explains His Joke	The Bakery
On the Day Pat Quinn Told Me [...]	The Bakery
Fair Warning	Foundling Review
Don't Believe Anything I Say	Linden Avenue Literary Journal
Anyone Worth Doing is Worth Doing Madly	Linden Avenue Literary Journal
Circumstantial Evidence	Linden Avenue Literary Journal
Two Things	Word Riot
The Rapist Stood Up in Court	Drunk in a Midnight Choir
What I Mean by Legacy	Drunk in a Midnight Choir
Cinders and All	Drunk in a Midnight Choir

Additionally, I'd like to thank the countless members of the Chicago and national poetry community who supported my work over the years. Thanks to Tim Stafford, Sara Eve Daly, Sean Patrick Mulroy, and Stevie Edwards. I am especially grateful to Stephanie Lane Sutton, Cynthia French, Team Mental Graffiti 2013, and Adriana E. Ramirez and Jesse Welch at Blue Sketch Press for believing in this book.

About the Author

Amy David is a poet and performer from Chicago, Illinois. She has represented Chicago four times at the national poetry slam, most recently on the 2013 semifinalist Team Mental Graffiti. Her work has appeared in journals including *Word Riot, Foundling Review, The Bakery, Shitcreek Review, Super Arrow, The Legendary, Full of Crow, Drunk in a Midnight Choir,* and *Linden Avenue Literary Journal,* as well as been anthologized in *Alight: The Best Loved Poems of WOWPS 2013* and Write Bloody's *We Will Be Shelter.*

www.ingramcontent.com/pod-product-compliance
Lightning Source LLC
Chambersburg PA
CBHW021449080526
44588CB00009B/755